Galileo Galilei
A LIFE OF CURIOSITY

by Jennifer Boothroyd

Lerner Publications Company • Minneapolis

Photo Acknowledgments

The images in this book are used with the permission of: Digital Vision Royalty Free, p. 4; © Mary Evans Picture Library, pp. 6, 23; © Erich Lessing/Art Resource, NY, p. 8; © Scala/Art Resource, NY, p. 9; © Sabina Bernacchini, IMSS-Florence, p. 10; © The Bridgeman Art Library/Getty Images, p.11; © The Granger Collection, New York, pp. 12, 15, 26; © SuperStock, Inc./SuperStock, p. 14; © Getty Images, pp. 16, 24; © Ann Ronan Picture Library/HIP/The Image Works, p. 18; © North Wind Picture Archives, p. 19; © Peter Willi/SuperStock, p. 20; © Victoria & Albert Museum, London/Art Resource, NY, p. 22; © The Art Archive/Sta Croce Florence/Dagli Orti (A), p. 25.

Cover: © Stock Montage/Getty Images.

Lerner Publications Company
A division of Lerner Publishing Group, Inc.
241 First Avenue North
Minneapolis, MN 55401 U.S.A.

Website address: www.lernerbooks.com

Words in **bold type** are explained in a glossary on page 31.

Library of Congress Cataloging-in-Publication Data

Boothroyd, Jennifer, 1972–
    Galileo Galilei : a life of curiosity / by Jennifer Boothroyd.
      p. cm. – (Pull ahead books)
    Includes bibliographical references and index.
    ISBN-13: 978–0–8225–6460–7 (lib. bdg. : alk. paper)
    ISBN-10: 0–8225–6460–2 (lib. bdg. : alk. paper)
     1. Galilei, Galileo, 1564–1642. 2. Astronomers–Italy–Biography–Juvenile literature.
   3. Inquiry (Theory of knowledge)–Juvenile literature. 4. Curiosity--Juvenile literature. I. Title.
   QB36.G2B626 2007
   520.92–dc22 [B]   2006024931

Manufactured in the United States of America
2 – JR – 9/1/09

Table of Contents

4

Questions

Why is the sky blue? How do birds fly? These may be questions you have asked. Some people are very **curious**. They want to learn about the world. Galileo Galilei was curious. He had many questions about the world. He worked all his life to find the answers.

Galileo taught at this school.

Looking for Answers

Galileo Galilei was born on February 15, 1564. He and his family lived in Italy. As a boy, Galileo liked math. He was also curious about science. He liked to learn how things worked. When Galileo grew up, he became a teacher. He taught math and science.

Galileo was also an inventor. He invented tools to help people learn about the world.

These are some of the tools that Galileo invented.

He made a thermometer to measure
temperature.

He made a balance so he could weigh
objects in water.

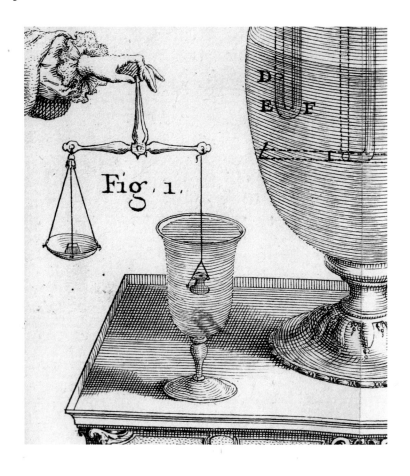

He made a **pendulum**. The hanging weight would swing back and forth. Galileo measured time by this motion.

This statue shows Galileo holding a pendulum.

Seeing Is Believing

In 1609, Galileo heard about a new invention. It was called a **telescope**. The telescope was a tube with glass **lenses** inside. A person could look through it and see things that were far away. Galileo made several telescopes of his own. He made each one stronger so he could see things farther away.

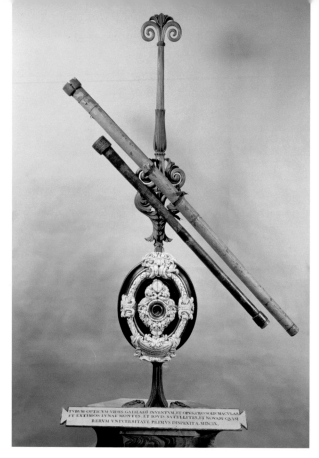

These are two of the telescopes that Galileo used.

With his new telescope, Galileo could see the moon and planets close up.

He learned that Jupiter had four moons.
He could also see that the **surface** of
Earth's moon was rough.

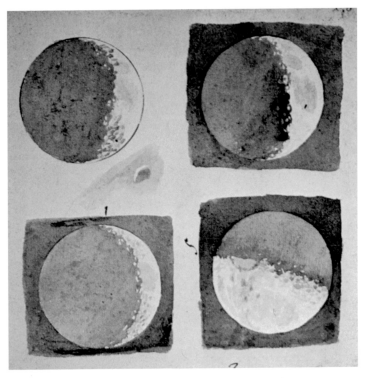

Galileo made these drawings of Earth's moon.

Copernicus

An Old Idea

Galileo learned about a scientist named Copernicus. Back then, most people believed that Earth was at the center of the **solar system**. Copernicus did not agree. He said that the Sun was at the center and that all the planets moved around it. But Copernicus could not prove his idea.

With his telescope, Galileo could see
how the planets moved in space. They
appeared to move around the Sun.
Copernicus was right!

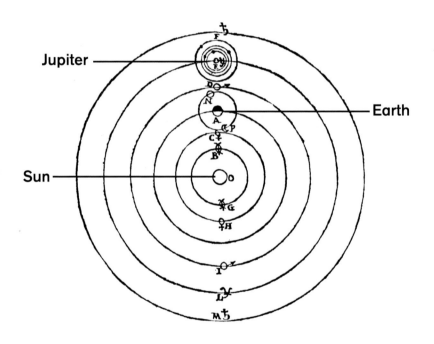

Galileo believed the solar system looked like this.

Many people were excited by Galileo's
discovery. But others were angry.

Galileo spoke to church leaders.

Who Is Right?

Many people in Galileo's time did not go to school. But they did go to church. Most people learned about the world from church leaders. People who did not believe what the leaders said could be punished.

The church leaders believed that Earth was at the center of the solar system.

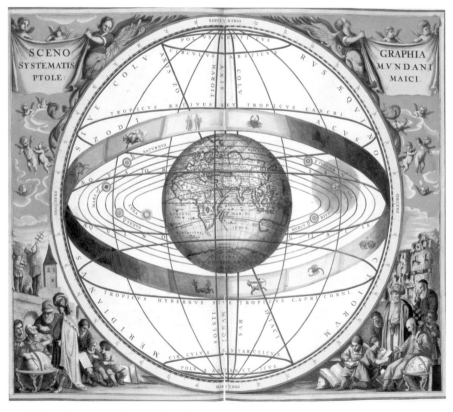

This drawing shows the Sun and planets moving around Earth.

They forced Galileo to say his idea was wrong. They arrested him.

Galileo apologizes to the church leaders.

This did not stop Galileo's curiosity.
He still had many questions.

He continued to search for the answers until he died in 1642.

Galileo's grave

Finding the Answers

Galileo wanted to learn about the world. He did not believe everything people told him. Galileo worked to find his own answers to his questions. His curiosity helped him make many important discoveries.

GALILEO GALILEI TIMELINE

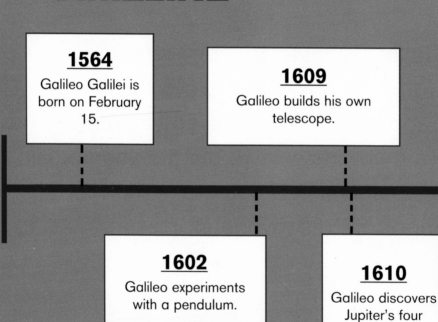

1564
Galileo Galilei is born on February 15.

1609
Galileo builds his own telescope.

1602
Galileo experiments with a pendulum.

1610
Galileo discovers Jupiter's four moons.

1633

Galileo is sent to jail.

1642

Galileo dies on January 8.

1641

Galileo designs a pendulum clock.

1800s

Most people agree with Galileo and Copernicus that Earth moves around the Sun.

More About Galileo Galilei

● Galileo designed a tool to solve math problems. It is called a compass. He made money selling the compass, a book of instructions, and lessons on how to use it.

● Galileo was good at math and science, but he was not perfect. Other scientists proved that some of Galileo's ideas about motion and ocean tides were wrong.

● In 1637, a sickness caused Galileo to become blind. Even after losing his eyesight, he designed a pendulum clock and wrote a book about motion.

Websites

The Galileo Games
http://www.pbs.org/wgbh/nova/pisa/galileo.html

Hero History
http://www.imahero.com/herohistory/galileo_herohistory.htm

NASA Quest
http://quest.nasa.gov/galileo/About/galileobio.html

Glossary

curious: excited to find out about something

discovery: something found or learned

lenses: curved pieces of clear glass

pendulum: a hanging weight that swings back and forth

solar system: the Sun, the planets, and their moons; everything that moves around the Sun

surface: the outside of an object

telescope: a tool used to see things that are far away

temperature: how warm or cool something is

Index